a gift for

Donna

love *from*

Wendy xxx

FRIENDS

with love

M·I·L·K

MOMENTS INTIMACY LAUGHTER KINSHIP

Many people will walk in and out of your life,
but only true friends will leave footprints in your heart.

[ELEANOR ROOSEVELT]

Every good thing is better if you can share it with a friend.

[PAM BROWN]

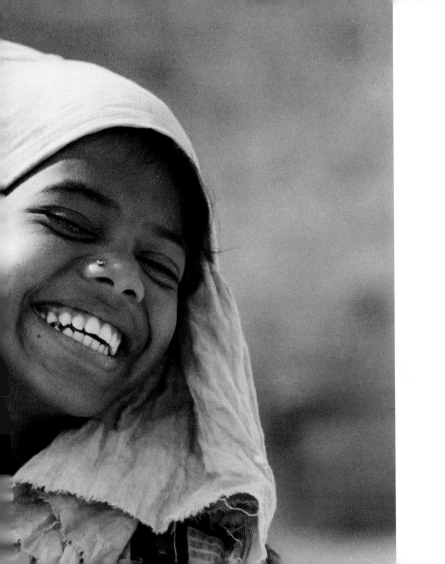

Friendship is
a **sheltering** tree.

[SAMUEL TAYLOR COLERIDGE]

Laughter is the shortest distance between two people.

[VICTOR BORGE]

Some people move our souls to dance.

[UNKNOWN]

Happiness seems **made** to be shared.

[JEAN RACINE]

Good times made better and bad times forgotten
due to the healing magic of friendship.

[MAEVE BINCHY]

Friends are all that matter.

[GELETT BURGESS]

The best and most **beautiful** things in the world cannot be seen or even touched. They must be felt with the heart.

[HELEN ADAMS KELLER]

In my friend,
I find a second self.

[ISABEL NORTON]

Friendship is what shows us
that we are **not alone**
in any joy or any sorrow.

[PAM BROWN]

There is no desire so deep as the simple desire

for companionship.

[GRAHAM GREENE]

There is such a difference between being a little daft all on your own
– and being a little daft together.

[PAM BROWN]

Friendship can only be measured

in memories, laughter, $peace$ and love.

[STUART AND LINDA MACFARLANE]

Kind words can be short
and easy to speak
but their echoes are truly endless.

When they are **real**,
friendships are not glass threads
or frost-work,
but the solidest thing we know.

[RALPH WALDO EMERSON]

Don't walk in front of me, I may not follow.
Don't walk behind me, I may not lead.
Just walk beside me
and be my friend.

[ALBERT CAMUS]

Page 2
© David M Grossman, USA
Six-year-old Ethan gives four-year-old Emory an enthusiastic hug at a birthday party in Brooklyn, New York.

Page 5
© Janice Rubin, USA
Six-year-old dancers Natasha and Mitalee look to each other for confidence before performing in front of a capacity crowd at the Houston International Festival, Texas, USA.

Page 6
© Cristina Piza, Germany
Musicians and old friends Ruben and Ibrahin celebrate the release of their new CD at a café in Madrid, Spain.

Page 7
© Paul Knight, New Zealand
In the small, bustling town of Wajima in Japan, a local resident is eager to pass on the latest news to her friend.

Pages 8–9
© Surendra Pradhan, India
Amid the paddy fields of rural India, the faces of two young workers are illuminated by laughter and friendship.

Pages 10–11
© Dilip Padhi, India
In a small village near Sambalpur, India, two young companions share a pensive moment.

Page 12
© David Williams, UK
Deckchairs on the pier provide a typical holiday setting for three friends taking a break in Brighton, in the south of England.

Page 14 and back cover
© Lori Carr, USA
Body paint and childhood imagination bond young warriors Billy and Shaun in San Rafael, California, USA.

Pages 15
© Amit Bar, The Netherlands
A comfortable sofa is the ideal spot for three-year-olds Allon and Tom to share laughter and play. The young friends live at the Kfar Hamaccabi Kibbutz in Israel.

Pages 16–17
© John Kaplan, USA
Double happiness – as Xia Yongqing, 84, and his nephew Yang Ziyun, 82, share a joke in the village of Nanyang in the Sichuan province of China.

Page 18
© Vladimir Kryukov, Russia
After a swim in the chilly waters of a Moscow river, a Russian couple steal the show with a display of affection.

Page 19
© Rachel Pfotenhauer, USA
Surrounded by their family, Jean and Paul celebrate their 50th wedding anniversary at Lake Tahoe, California, USA. Reunited for this special occasion, their children and grandchildren dance in circles around the delighted couple.

Page 20
© Katherine Fletcher, USA
Wedded bliss in Omaha, Nebraska, USA – inhibitions are shed as new bride Stephanie and her friends get into party mood.

Page 21
© Yorghos Kontaxis, USA
Coney Island in New York, USA – six friends turn a sandy beach into a dance floor to the delight of their enthusiastic audience.

Page 22
© K Hatt, USA
Free fall – four bikini-clad friends leap off a pier into the water below in Miami, Florida, USA.

Page 23
© Tetsuaki Oda, Japan
Two children are happy to amuse themselves during the interval of an outdoor music concert in Linköping, Sweden.

Pages 24–25
© Damrong Juntawonsup, Thailand
In a rural village in the Chiangrai province of Thailand, children cheer home the winner of a running race.

Page 27
© Andreas Heumann, UK
Three young friends share the shelter of an umbrella as they wait patiently for an open-air rock concert to begin in London, England.

Pages 28–29
© Gay Block, USA
In the bright sunshine of Miami, Florida, two friends make sure their noses are well protected as they stroll arm in arm along South Beach.

Page 30
© Noelle Tan, USA
Bonnie's enthusiastic greeting is matched by a delighted smile from friend Nancy in Washington DC, USA.

Page 31
© Amelia Panico, USA
In New York, a compassionate and loving moment is shared between a young nurse, Susan, and her 97-year-old patient, Carolina.

Pages 32–33
© Jinjun Mao, China
In Shuinan village, China, the mischievous antics of a five-year-old visitor amuse and delight his grandfather and friends.

Page 35
© Nicholas Ross, UK
On a dusty pavement in the slums of Bombay, India, friendship blossoms for 12-year-old Indou and her blind companion, Mala.

Pages 36–37
© Zoe Ali, Australia
One Saturday afternoon on a state housing complex in Euston, London, England, the photographer captured a moment with two young neighbours.

Pages 38–39
© Francesca Mancini, Italy
United in grief – a moment of solidarity as a young Kosovan woman embraces her friend whose husband has been killed by a mine.

Page 40
© Greta Pratt, USA
Summer in New Jersey, USA – best friends Axel and Colby take a break from swimming to cool off with an ice cream.

Page 41
© Thierry Des Ouches, France
Young sun worshippers Diane and Audrey take it easy on the beach in Noirmoutier, France. Their photographer father captures the scene.

Page 42
© Malie Rich-Griffith, USA
Laughter is infectious for two friends from Mgahinga village, Uganda.

Page 43
© Thomas Patrick Kiernan, Ireland
Two Indian women walk side by side as they carry vegetables to market in Calcutta, India.

Page 45
© Robin Sparks Daugherty, USA
During a summer drought in New Mexico, USA, three friends prove that there is still fun to be had with only two inches of water in the pool.

Page 46
© Victor Englebert, USA
On Lakawon Island in the Philippines, local children sit in the rain outside their school. They pull their self-made toys on the basketball court – the island's only smooth surface available to them.

Page 47
© Victor Englebert, USA
A group of young girls cool off in an outdoor shower in Ghana.

Pages 48–49 and front cover
© Peter Gabriel, USA
A fashion-conscious trio discover the perfect accessory as they sit in a café in New York.

Pages 50–51
© Hank Willis Thomas, USA
Three friends compose their own picture within a picture at a Million Women March in Philadelphia, Pennsylvania, USA.

Page 52
© Marianne Thomas, USA
William Bossidy listens attentively to his friend John Noonan, a fellow resident at their nursing home in Florida, USA.

Pages 54–55
© Joan Sullivan, Canada
In the foothills of the Himalayas, a Nepalese grandfather looks after his two grandchildren while he catches up on news brought from Kathmandu by a young porter.

Pages 56–57
© Kailash Soni, India
Conversation comes easily to two old friends as they relax opposite the Shiv Temple of Bilawali in Dewas, India.

Page 58
© Pat Justis, USA
A country lane in Olympia, Washington, USA, becomes an adventurous path for childhood friends Keegan, aged six, and Graeme, seven.

Page 59
© Dharmesh Bhavsar, Canada
Free wheeling – a rolling wheel leads an energetic race for three companions on a deserted road in Baroda, India.

Page 61
© Michael Chiabaudo, USA
As his friends stride out along a dusty village street near Tijuana, Mexico, a young boy – and his trousers – try to keep up.